Car Stars
CHEVROLET

CORVETTE

Dash!
LEVELED READERS

2

Dash!
LEVELED READERS

Level 1 – Beginning
Short and simple sentences with familiar words or patterns for children who are beginning to understand how letters and sounds go together.

Level 2 – Emerging
Longer words and sentences with more complex language patterns for readers who are practicing common words and letter sounds.

Level 3 – Transitional
More developed language and vocabulary for readers who are becoming more independent.

abdopublishing.com

Published by Abdo Zoom, a division of ABDO, P.O. Box 398166, Minneapolis, Minnesota 55439.
Copyright © 2018 by Abdo Consulting Group, Inc. International copyrights reserved in all countries.
No part of this book may be reproduced in any form without written permission from the publisher.

Printed in the United States of America, North Mankato, Minnesota.
092017
012018

Photo Credits: Alamy, AP Images, iStock, Shutterstock
Production Contributors: Kenny Abdo, Jennie Forsberg, Grace Hansen, John Hansen
Design Contributors: Dorothy Toth, Neil Klinepier

Publisher's Cataloging in Publication Data
Names: Murray, Julie, author.
Title: Chevrolet Corvette / by Julie Murray.
Description: Minneapolis, Minnesota: Abdo Zoom, 2018. | Series: Car stars |
    Includes online resource and index.
Identifiers: LCCN 2017939238 | ISBN 9781532120794 (lib.bdg.) | ISBN 9781532121913 (ebook) |
    ISBN 9781532122477 (Read-to-Me ebook)
Subjects: LCSH: Chevrolet Corvette--Juvenile literature. | Vehicles--Juvenile literature. | Cars--Juvenile
    literature.
Classification: DDC 629.2222--dc23
LC record available at https://lccn.loc.gov/2017939238

Table of Contents

Chevrolet Corvette

The Corvette is a popular **sports car**. It is an American **classic**.

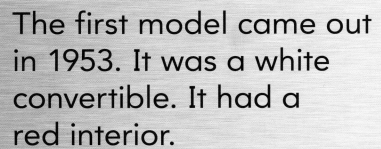

The first model came out in 1953. It was a white convertible. It had a red interior.

Since then, many other models have been made. The Stingray came out in 1963. It quickly became a popular car.

Many people like the ZR1. It can go more than 200 mph (322 kph)!

The Look

The Corvette has rounded edges. The front is long. The back is short. It sits low to the ground.

It is made for two. It has two doors. It only has two seats.

It has a rear-opening hood.
A **V8** engine powers it.

The 2017 Z06 has 650 **horsepower**. It can go from 0-60 mph (0-96.5 kph) in 2.9 seconds!

People like corvettes! They are fun to drive. They also have a lower price tag than most **sports cars**. The 2017 Grand Sport starts at $67,000.

The Corvette is also a racing car. The C7.R has won many times.

More Facts

- The Chevy Corvette is named after corvette warships.

- The first model sold for $3,498.

- It is the longest American made **sports car** (1953-present).

Glossary

classic – something that remains popular over a long period of time.

horsepower – a unit of power that equals the work done in lifting 550 pounds one foot in one second.

sports car – a low-built car designed for performance at high speeds.

V8 – an engine with 8 cylinders mounted on the crankcase.

Index

Online Resources

Booklinks
NONFICTION NETWORK
FREE! ONLINE NONFICTION RESOURCES

To learn more about Corvettes, please visit **abdobooklinks.com**. These links are routinely monitored and updated to provide the most current information available.